The Power Of God's Grace

By Modupe Thompson

The Power Of God's Grace
ISBN 1 902443 15 9

Published by CTW Productions
P O Box 25026
London SW4 6WG UK

Cover Design by *Him*Pressions

Unless otherwise indicated, all scripture quotations are taken
from the King James Version of the Bible.

TABLE OF CONTENTS

ACKNOWLEDGMENT

First of all, I acknowledge the Almighty God, the Son and the Holy Spirit who stayed with me and inspired me in the course of this book, may His name be praised.

Gratefully, I recognise my husband and my children for their support and their patience.

I also acknowledge my brothers and sisters in the Lord for the typing of the manuscript at the various stages. The Bible says *"how good and pleasant it is for brethren to dwell together in unity."* Thank you very much for your love and support.

INTRODUCTION

This book is written to demonstrate the love of God to mankind. God is love (I John 4: 8). He is good and His mercies endure forever. He called everything into existence through His love. Omnipotent, Omniscient and Omnipresent — God is immortal, infallible and the essence of love.

John 1: 1-3 says *"in the beginning, the Word existed, He was with God and He was God. He was in the beginning with God and He created everything."*

As God's creation, we are all valuable and unique. Apart from God we are nothing, and if we try to live without him, we will abandon the purpose for which we were made.

Genesis 1:1 says, *"in the beginning God created the heavens and the earth."* Thus, He existed before creation and expands beyond it. His benevolent intent in creating all things good and perfect reveals His Holy nature. By virtue of creation, all kingdom, power and authority flows through him.

There was a time when God started to create the beginning; and one day the time will come when the world will come to an end. God is not using the clock of this world because He is outside of time. He upholds creation and time. God's wonderful creation will only be completed when Christ the Lord comes in full glory at the end of the world. As our day started with beginning, God has no beginning, end, past, present, and no future.

God is the supreme Creator and Lord. Humankind is made in His image to worship Him.

Oh Lord you live forever, long ago you created the earth and with your own hands you made the heavens. You are a loving God. You made us in your image — to know and love You. Oh Lord our God how majestic is your name.

CHAPTER 1

GOD IN CREATION

In the beginning was the word, and the word was with God, and the word was God. He was in the beginning with God. All things were made through Him, and without Him nothing was made that was made. In Him was life, and the life was the light of men. And the light shines in the darkness, and the darkness did not comprehend it.

John 1:5 (NIV)

The Word is Jesus Christ, the eternal. In the beginning the Bible says in Genesis 1, the earth was without form and void, it lacked order and darkness was on the face of the deep. God is a God of order and He brought all things into being in an orderly manner.

Through the spoken Word of God, light came to being and darkness disappeared. Two masters cannot be in the boat; one would have to retreat. Darkness was rebuked and rendered powerless from the beginning. Where God is, darkness will have to flee.

Darkness stands for evil, problem and chaos, but God in His divine power transformed the chaos through His outstretched hands — the Holy Spirit, His executive arm.

God spoke the world into existence and things were created through Him.

> For by him all things were created, that are in heaven, visible and invisible, whether they be thrones, or dominions, or principalities or power: all things were created by him, and for him.

Colossians 1:16 (KJV)

Every creation of God was very good, perfectly made, whole and spotless.

> Then God said, let us make man in our image, according to our likeness: let them have dominion over the fish of the sea, over the birds of the air, and over all the earth and over every creeping things that creeps on the earth, So God created man in his own image, in the image of God created him, male and female he created them.
>
> And God blessed them and said to them, be fruitful and multiply; fill the earth and subdue it; have dominion over the fish of the sea, the birds of the air, and every living creature that moves upon the earth.

Genesis 1:26-28 (NKJV)

Man's power and authority originated in God's intent to make man in his own image and likeness. Man is distinct from the rest of God's creation. The divine triune counsel determined that man should be created in God's image. Thus man is a spiritual being who not only has a body but also a soul and Spirit. He is a moral being whose intelligence, perception and self-determination forever exceeds that of any other earthly being. The properties and traits attributed to mankind and his prominence in the order of the creation imply the intrinsic worth, not only to Adam and Eve but also to all mankind.

As creatures of God, we can see, think, sense and reason. Man has five sensory organs. The Bible stated how God formed everything from the ground, all the beast of the field and all the birds of the air and brought them to the man to see what he would name them, and whatever man called each living creature that was its name (Genesis 2:19). God certainly loved man even before He made him that He gave him dominion over all His works and put all things under his feet.

Man in his desire to know everything forfeited the authority bestowed on him. Scientists have come up with all sorts of research into creation, they have gone into outer space searching for the power that holds the planet. No one can grasp the infinite wisdom of God and no man can fathom the depth of His love for us. No one knows the mind of God except the Holy Spirit, the Counsellor.

When I consider your heavens, the work of your fingers, the moon and the stars, which you have ordained, what Is man that you are mindful of him, and son of man that you

visit him? For you have made him a little lower than the
angels, and you have crowned him with glory and honour.

Psalms 8:3-6 (KJV)

God covered us with glory and splendour; we were
spotless and wholesome. No wonder Psalm139:14 says
"we are wonderfully made by God".

And the Lord God formed man of the dust of the ground,
and breathed into his nostrils, the breath of life; and man
became a living being.

Genesis 2:7 (NKJV)

God gave mankind a precious life. Isn't that
wonderful? God made man and put him in the Garden
of Eden to till it. He also gave him a helpmate to assist
man in his work. The Lord God then commanded man
saying *"of every tree of the garden you may freely eat but of
the tree of the knowledge of good and evil you shall not eat, for
the day that you eat you shall die."*

God placed His trust in man giving him a free will.
Despite this He knows our weakness and capabilities,
therefore he warned man. What a great warning! The
authority given to man and the warning was a covenant
between man and God an accepted binding agreement.

Genesis 3:18 says *"and they heard the sound of the Lord
God walking in the garden, in the cool of the day. Adam and
Eve hid themselves from the presence of the Lord God."*
You will begin to wonder why Adam and Eve hid from

God, despite their closeness and intimacy with Him, I'll tell you why.

One night after they had eaten and were resting, the tempter came into the mind of the woman to have a taste of the tree which God had warned them not to eat. The tempter says *"Has God indeed said, you shall not eat of every tree of the garden?"* (Genesis 3:1-3). The tempter suggested "you could have more!" Through satan's influence, Eve shifted her focus from all that God had done and given to the one thing He had withheld. Eve was willingly accepting satan's offer without checking with God. Sound familiar? How often is our attention drawn from the much which is ours to the little that isn't? "I've got to have it." Eve is typical of us all. And we consistently show that we are her descendants by repeating her mistakes.

She fell into temptation. We must realise that being tempted is not a sin. We have not sinned until we give into the temptation. But what can I do to resist the tempter?

(1) Pray for the strength to resist,

(2) Flee,

(3) Say "no" when confronted with what is wrong,

(4) Lastly, we need to keep God's Word in our
decision making.

The Bible is our guide book, God says *"if we are willing and obedient we shall eat the best of the land."* Whenever you struggle to figure out things and feel sorry for yourself about what you don't have, consider all you do have and start thanking God then He'll help you kill the giant man in your life (I Samuel 17:32-37).

The first man sold the authority, power, dominion and the entire inheritance God placed in his hands to the devil. They were left with nothing. Man was first covered with the glory of God, but his disobedience left him in shame. Man fell from grace to grass through food. If you obey your Creator you will be blessed there is no two side to it.

> Let us hear the conclusion of the whole matter: fear the Lord and keep His commandments for this is the whole duty of all men.
>
> **Ecclesiastes12:13 (NKJV)**

Obedience is better than sacrifice. We must learn from people's mistakes, whilst being careful not to be judgmental or blaming others or else it is easy to fall into the same temptation. We need to call for the help of the Holy Spirit in prayer to resist the tempter, He alone can help us (John 14-16)

You may questions about the devil. Did God create him? Why is he so powerful and able to carry on deceiving people to this day? I hope you would be pleased to know that satan was not created to be devil. He is a spirit. satan was once a cherub standing before the presence of the Lord God. He was a senior choir leader that led the angels and other living creatures before God in singing Holy, Holy until sin was found in him. He wanted to be like God.

> How are you fallen from heaven o Lucifer, son of the morning star! How are you cut down to the ground, you who are weakened the nations; for you have said in your heart, I will ascend into heaven. I will exalt my throne above the stars of God. I will also sit on the mount of the congregation, on the farthest sides of the north, the clouds. I will be like the most high.
>
> Isaiah 14: 12-15 (NKJV)

(Hear the reply of the highest) *satan you will be brought down to the soil, to the depth of the pit.* satan was cast down to the earth. A fallen person will not wish anybody to stand or to obey the commandment of God. From the time of his fall, satan started looking for everywhere to destroy the work of his Creator. The fundamental sin of satan was pride. Five times in the quoted scripture he said; *"I will..."* This led him to rebellion and self-sufficiency. God resists the proud and gives grace to the humble.

Man fell from grace to grass.

> Now the serpent was the shrewdest of all the creatures the Lord God had made. "Really?"he asked the woman. "Did God really say you must not eat any of the fruit in the garden?"

"Of course we may eat it" the woman told him. It's only the fruit from the centre of the garden that we are not allowed to eat. God says we must not eat or even touch it, or we will die."

"You won't die!" the serpent hissed. "God knows your eyes will opened when you eat it. You will become just like God, knowing everything, both good and evil."

The woman was convinced. The fruit looked so fresh and delicious, and it would make her wise! So she ate some of the fruit. She also gave some to her husband who was with her. Then he too ate it.

Genesis 3:1-6 (NLT)

We can see that Eve had lost the battle from the onset. First she saw it, took it and gave it. The battle is often lost at the first look. Temptation often begins by simple seeing something you want.

The woman saw that the fruit of the tree was good and pleasing to the eye and desirable for gaining wisdom. She took some and ate; she also gave some to her husband. After eating of the fruits of the tree of life they both realised they were naked. They sewed leaves together and made coverings for themselves. This indicates self righteousness compared to the glory of God that first covered them. Likewise anybody without Christ is naked, empty, lonely. and covered with darkness.

Adam and Eve's newly gained awareness did not bring them the promise or knowledge of good but evil and embarrassment over their nakedness. They now hid themselves from the King of glory who Sees.

Satan used a sincere motive to tempt Eve — You will be like god, he lied. It wasn't wrong of Eve to want to be like God, to become more like God is humanity's highest goal. It must be our desire, but satan always comes in another way by deceiving us into defying the authority of God. He wants us to take God's place. Self-exaltation leads to rebellion against God. satan will make sin desirable and pleasant to you — the pleasant sins are the hardest to avoid but by the grace of God there is a way of escape (I Corinthians 10:13)

The Lord called Adam and said, *"where are you?"* Adam certainly did not give a direct answer neither did his wife, Eve. Instead of admitting their faults they decided to blame each other. Do you see yourself in a situation where you never admit any wrongdoing, but blame your faults on others? It is better to accept and admit your faults. When you do, you would be more at peace and it would be well with you. Think of whatever you do, if it seems appealing, dreadful or shameful, desist from doing it, for the love of God is so much. As God loved the first Adam and placed all His works in his hands likewise His love for you — through His Son Jesus — has put you back in your rightful place (Psalms 139:7).

God loves you but hates your act of sin. For you to have a right relationship with him and to keep from running when no one pursues, give all to him.

Romans 5:12-14 says therefore just as through one man sin entered the world and death spread to all men. Sin is like a sickness without cure. It spreads like cancer, and only the Great Physician — the Creator —can cure it. Until the law, sin was in the world but sin is not imputed when there is no law. Nevertheless death reigned from Adam to Moses even over those who had not sinned according to the likeness of the transgression of Adam who is a type of him who was to come.

But the gift is not like the offence. For if, many died by the offence of one man, how much more did God's grace and the gift that came by the grace of the one man, Jesus Christ, overflow to the many! Again, the gift of God is not like the result of the one man's sin: The judgement followed one sin and brought condemnation, but the gift followed many trespasses and brought justification.

Adam was our representative. Adam as a type of Christ (I Corinthians 15:22). *"For as in Adam all died so in Christ all will be made alive."*

Adam and Christ are similar in the fact that their deeds have affected many people. However, the differences are more pronounced. Christ's deed was of grace resulting in justification and life, whereas Adam's deed was of sin resulting in condemnation and death. Adam was characterised by disobedience whereas Christ was characterised by obedience. All mankind are in Adam by birth, but in Christ by faith.

Judgement on mankind and the devil

And I will put enmity between thee and the woman and between thy seed and her seed; it shall bruise thy head, and thou shall bruise his heel.

Genesis 3:15 (KJV)

God never brought Himself so low to the devil to ask any question. He went straight and pronounced his judgement upon him. The curse to the devil has a broader application interpreted messianically. Enmity represents conflict between satan, "thy seed" and "her seed" came to pass when our Lord Jesus was born.

...but when the fullness of the time was come, God sent forth his son made of a woman made under the law.

Galatians 4: 4 (KJV)

This was fulfiled in Jesus the seed through Virgin Mary (Luke 1:26-35). God promised to bring the Redeemer from the seed of the woman, that Jesus — completely human and divinely begotten — would be at war with the serpent. Jesus would smite him and make him a public spectacle of the power of hell.

...and having spoiled principalities and power he made a shew of them openly triumphing over them in it.

Colossians 2:15 (KJV)

God turned to man and his wife pronouncing His judgement upon them. **To the woman He said,** *"l will greatly multiply thy sorrow and thy conception; in sorrow thou shall bring forth children, and thy desire shall be to thy husband, and he shall rule over thee."* Conception means pain in child bearing and is still to this day. The Bible says, *"heaven and the earth shall pass away but my word shall not come back to me except it does what l sent it to do".* You can see what disobedience has caused for us mankind.

To the man God said *"because you are the cause of the whole thing thou has hearkened unto the voice of thy wife, and hast eaten of the tree of which l commanded you saying "thou shalt not eat of it" cursed is the ground for thy sake. In sorrow shalt thou eat of it all the day of your life; for out of it wast thou shall eat the herb of the field. In the sweat of thy face shalt thou eat bread, till thou return to the ground; out of it wast thou taken; for dust thou art and dust shalt thou return."*

Here we are, we lost the wholeness of God's dominion and spiritual knowledge, which is revelational spiritual senses and we received instead physical knowledge.

We lost authority and power and gave the key of the kingdom to the devil, the serpent. Glory to God in whom weakness is not found, from the beginning of the earth God loved the people He made.

After He cursed, He clothed man and woman with garments made with skins of animal. The blood of that animal was shed for a covering. This substitutionary atonement points to our Lord Jesus. From the above reading can you see the role of man in the affair of the earth?

God loves us; we are the sheep of his pasture. He made us in his image and placed everything He made in our hands to enjoy, live without problems and to be in good harmony with him. Can we blame God for what He has done? Was He not fair enough by setting everything in order? As the owner of my properties, I decided to place my driver to be the Lord over all things but one of my cars. The driver was very pleased with my words, but after he had eaten and was overfed, he forgot our agreement. What do you think will happen to the unfaithful servant? Ponder on it and judge the two of us. That was exactly what happened between God and Adam.

Unless there is repentance, anyone that sins will surely die. Let us look at one of the faithful servants whose master placed in the trusted position of second in command. His name was Joseph.

> **Then pharaoh said to Joseph "in as much as God has shown you all these there is no one as discerning and wise as you you shall be over my house and all my people shall be ruled according to your word only in regard to the throne will I be greater than you."**
>
> **Genesis 41:39-40 (NKJV)**

As we read in the Bible Joseph was faithful in all his deeds and his master was very pleased with him. Joseph was a type of Jesus Christ who, being in very nature of

God did not consider equality with God something to be grasped, but made himself nothing, taking the very nature of a servant, being made in human likeness, And being found in appearance as a man he humbled himself and became obedient to the death even death on a cross! His will is to obey his father. What about you?

Joseph was tempted by the devil through the lust of the eyes again, but glory to God in the highest, he did not fail nor fall. Because of the nature of God that was in him, and the fact that he had been feeding on the Word of God, he was given the stability to resist the devilish attempts of his master's wife.

(Genesis 39:6-9) *"Thus he left all that he had in Joseph's hand and he did not know what he had except for the bread which he ate. Now Joseph was handsome in form and appearance. And it came to pass after these things that his master's wife cast longing eyes on Joseph and she said, "lie with me." But he refused and said to his master's wife, "look my master does not know what is with me in his house and he has committed all that he has with to my hand. There is no one greater in this house nor has he kept back anything from me but you, because you are his how can I do this great wickedness, and sin against God?"*

Joseph knew his boundaries and did not trespass. Temptation is not a sin but yielding to it will cause problem, which we are still facing from the time of Adam and Eve. There is a proverb that says 'there is no barn that has no designation.' God gave you everything to enjoy. God is love evil is not found in Him. Joseph loved the God of his fathers and feared no man. Though he suffered for injustice God delivered him and he was covered with the glory of God and Joseph prospered, our Lord Jesus did the same for us. All of us have gone astray like a sheep that has no shepherd through Adam. The Judgements of the Lord are true and righteous altogether.

Adam and Eve sold their birth right to the devil and made bad bargain with their lives just because of food and the lust of the eyes. Esau was one of the sons of Jacob, he was supposed to be the prince, but because of food he sold himself to his brother and made a bad bargain with his life. He could not get back his birthright.

What an irreversible damage he did to his life. Esau suffered for it, likewise anybody without the grace of God is still in Adam and that person is making a bad bargain with his or her life. Life is more than money or gold and silver. Genesis 25:29-32 says once when Jacob was cooking some stew, Esau came in from open country, famished. He said to Jacob," Quick let me have some of that red stew! I'm famished" (that is why he was called Edom). Jacob replied, "first sell me your birth right." "Look, I am about to die." Esau said, "what good is birthright to me." He sold himself for short term satisfaction. The book of Hebrew says, Esau who for a single meal sold his inheritance rights as the oldest son, afterwards, as you know, when he wanted to inherit this blessing he was rejected. He could bring about no change of mind, though he sought the blessing with tears.

God gave all to you through His Son, come out of Adam and don't trade your birthright for you not to regret later. God is real.

Man's role in the affairs of the earth.

From the perspective of man's strategic role we must assume man to be more valuable than anything on earth. No other form of earthly life plays such a cosmic role. The world literally stands or falls based on the actions of man, only man has the power to deplete the earth's resources and pollute it's atmosphere.

The sin of one man — Adam — corrupted the world, the continued sinfulness of one man caused the flood. (Genesis 6:11-12) *"The earth also was corrupt and filled with violence. So God looked upon the earth, and indeed it was corrupt. For all flesh had corrupted their way on the earth."*

In contrast of the obedience of one man — Jesus Christ — brought justification. Think about it, should we blame God for all what He has done for us? He made us in His own image, He gave man blessing to rule over all things, over the fish of the sea and bird of the air and over all living creature that move on the ground and multiply in child bearing (receive yours today if you are waiting on the Lord in Jesus name.)

God is good regardless of all we've done, He is still looking for every way to redeem mankind. He sent another man named Noah; then Abraham, prophets, judges and kings but men ignored Him even some say there is no God. Some believe there is a God but do not know how to reach Him. Others believe in God but not in His Son Jesus Christ, that he sent to save the whole world for the Bible says no one can see the father except through the Son (John 6-44). God is calling everyone to repentance not because of our goodness but His mercy.

Consequence of sin

For the wages of sin is death, but the gift of God is eternal life in Christ Jesus our Lord.

Romans 6: 23 (NKJV)

Immediately sin entered the world through one man sadness, loneliness, sickness, physical death, separation came into the world. The world once filled with goodness — a place without blame — now was filled with darkness. But there is a way out for you, the gift of God is eternal life receive it and live. Stop putting blame on your parents. Some say if there is God why do people become sick or die of hunger. Remember the earth has been cursed.

Cursed is the ground for your sake in toil you shall eat of it all the days of your life.

Genesis 3:17 (NKJV)

Thus life-long struggle will end in death, Psalms 104:14 declares that He causes the grass to grow for the cattle and vegetable for service of man.

I recently spoke to a man in the hospital where I worked, this man was very ill he was taken from one hospital to another I witnessed about the goodness of God to him, he said to me "I know all about Jesus but I just find it very difficult to believe," he started cursing his parent and God.

You can not blame him for his lack of knowledge, he thought that his parent and God brought him to this world to suffer. Are you in that situation today? I am telling you today, there is no solution anywhere than God the Giver of life, it's all about choices.

CHAPTER TWO

GOD'S COVENANT WITH MANKIND

For God so loved the world and gave his one and only son, that whoever believes in him shall not perish but have eternal life.

John 3:16 (NIV)

God loved the world and gave His Son to every tongue and tribe both white and black, prostitute, backslider and drug addict. Before our Lord Jesus came, God has been looking for a way to rescue mankind by making covenants with some people.

God wants to reveal His truth and beauty to the world. When God made the heavens and the earth, he made man in his own likeness. God sent Adam and Eve out of the garden after their disobedience. They met together and gave birth to two sons, and one of them sinned against God by murdering his own brother.

He was cursed as a result, after which they gave birth to a boy called Seth. Then man started calling upon the name of God. (Genesis 4:25-26) And Adam knew his wife again and bore a son and named him Seth, for God has appointed another seed for me instead of Abel whom Cain killed. As for Seth to him also son was born, and he named him Enoch. Then men began to call on the name of the Lord.

Seth was given to replace Abel, that Cain murdered, and through his blood line, we can trace the birth of our Lord Jesus Christ — see God's love. He makes his grace abound to us in a way we can not fathom. We can liken this to Hagar the maidservant of Sarah the Egyptian woman who gave birth to Ishmael through the grace of God (Genesis 16:1)

The psalmist says in Psalms 115:3 *"Our God is in heaven; he does whatever pleases him the other side says he does whatever pleases him in the heaven and on earth, in the seas and all their depths. No one can query Him"* Romans 11:13 says *"Esau I hated Jacob I love,"* that is the grace of God. He went further on to say. *"I will have mercy on whom I will have mercy upon and compassion on whom I will have compassion, will the thing formed say to him who formed it, "why have you made me like this."*

I want to let you know that God exercises his power Sovereignly in abundant mercy not in strict justice. The Word of God says, *"It is neither of him that wills nor of him who runs but God who shows mercy."* Yes they called God and worship Him and trusted in him as their power and their strength, but after eating and drinking out of what the Lord had given them they started doing what was evil before Him who sits on the throne. Out of them all we find one man who walked with God. His name was Enoch he walked with God and was taken away by God not to see corruption. Likewise, if you walk with the Lord you will not see evil, you walk over your enemies by the grace of God who made you in His own image.

After Enoch's rapture onto God, Enoch's the earth started doing evil. They built the towel of Babel, they wanted to see God. God was furious and pronounced his judgement and scattered their language . Before then, the Lord saw the wickedness of man was great in the earth and that every intent of the thoughts of his heart was only evil continually.

And the Lord was sorry that he made man on the earth and he was grieved in His heart so the Lord said, *"I will destroy man whom I have created from the face of the earth, both man and the beast, creeping things and the birds of the air, for I am sorry that I made them."* But Noah found grace in the eyes of the Lord. Grace means favour unconditional love which means no matter what you've done I will love you unconditionally.

Undeserved favour! What a mighty God we serve hallelujah. The book of Isaiah 49:15-16 declares *"can a mother forget the baby at her breast and have no compassion on the child she has borne? Though she may forget, I will not forget you! See, l have engraved you on the palms of my hands; your walls are ever before me."* This means even though we sin and break the heart of God, nevertheless He is still loving and gracious in mercy to mankind, so much that he will find a way to rescue his people (Jeremiah 31:3).

Noah opened his heart after him by God revealed Himself to him as the Creator of heaven and the earth. God told Noah, "go and witness to my people to repent from their wayward lives for I am coming to destroy the earth." They laughed at Noah the evangelist. They made jest of him and thought he was blaspheming not knowing that their own lives were at stake.

Noah's message was repent for the kingdom of God is at hand. This word is for you today, Jesus Christ is coming back. Read Acts 1:9-11, it says, when Jesus was taken from the earth to heaven the disciples were watching. Two angels from heaven appeared to them who also said, "*Men of Galilee, why do you stand gazing up into heaven? This Jesus who was taken up from you into heaven, will so come in like manner as you saw Him go into heaven*" thus confirms Jesus' return. I don't want you to be deceived by wrong doctrines, the scripture is God-breathed and is good for all doctrine.

Believe it and you will be saved. God made a covenant with Noah to spare his life and family. Noah hearkens to the voice of the Lord and starts witnessing to people about the flood. He witnessed for 120 years but they harden their hearts. They thought he was joking. Are we not like these people today despising the Lord? Take heed! People were drinking and merrying, giving children in marriage without fearing the Lord. But the Word of God still came to pass.

The covenant God had with Noah was to make an ark of gopher wood. (Genesis 6: 17) *"and behold, I myself am bringing flood waters on the earth, to destroy from under heaven all flesh in which is the breath of the life everything that is on the earth shall die but l will establish my covenant with you and you shall go into the ark, you, your sons, your wife, and your son's wives with you. And of every living thing of all flesh, you shall bring two of every sort into the ark to keep them alive with you; they shall be male and female."* What for? For God to start the new earth again after the flood. Isn't God wonderful?

He used water to wipe away sin making a new start. Noah was faithful by doing as God commanded him to do, till the day of the Lord came upon the earth and the flood swept away mankind. Noah, his household and some animals were spared as promised and God blessed them to be fruitful and multiply and fill the earth (Genesis 9: 1-6) God reaffirmed man's original dominion over the earth with Noah.

I want to let you know that a man's life is very sacred, every moving thing that lives shall be food even the green herbs but the Lord warned not to eat flesh with blood. God even said, surely for our lifeblood he will demand a reckoning; from the hand of every beast, and every hand of man from every man's brother I will require the life of a man who ever sheds man's blood. If you remember after God made man even in His own image in the likeness of him he breath the breath of life into his nostrils and man became a living being.

> **And the Lord God formed man of the dust of the ground, and breathed into his nostrils the breath of Life and man became a living being.**
>
> **Genesis 2:7 (NKJV)**

God declared from his whole office, The Trinity. *"Come let us make man in our own image."* Do you realise the number of man that God made "ONE" means uniqueness of God. You are unique and special in the hands of God. The woman was brought out from man and joined together and became one. That is why man has to leave his parents and cling to his wife and become one not two. You must see yourselves as one.

Man is God's kingdom agent to rule and subdue the earth and everything in it including the satanic forces. Man is God's unique spiritual, immortal and intelligent creation. God's blessing from the beginning is still the same for his people.

God now establishes His covenant with Noah that He will not destroy the earth with a flood again. He now gave a sign that will be everlasting between God and man.

> **Thus I will establish a covenant with you: never again shall there be a flood to destroy the earth.**
>
> **Genesis 9:11-19**

When God repeats words He means. As an unconditional promise to all that God will never again destroy the earth with flood, he left a sign behind that always amazes me whenever I see it.

And God said *"this is the sign of the covenant between you and me for perpetual generations. I have set my rainbow in the cloud and it shall be for the sign of covenant between me and the earth,"* not only Noah and his children but to the whole earth both white and black from generation to generations.

What do you think or feel about God when you see a rainbow ? When there has been some rain and the sun shines brightly, it happens naturally. Oh! What a wonderful sign to use. God always remembers his covenant with mankind.

Just like Jesus, when God sees the blood of his Son Jesus Christ He will remember and forgive you of your sin and set you apart. Noah lived after the flood three hundred and fifty years and they worshiped the Lord, but the flood has not neutralised the influence of the devil nor has it changed mankind's capacity for rebellion against God's rule.

Noah was a farmer and he planted a vineyard. Don't forget that God cursed Adam in Genesis 3:1-19, cursed is the ground for your sake in toil you shall eat of it all the days of your life. God's Word cannot change. Noah enjoyed the goodness of God but out of human frailty Noah got drunk (Genesis 9:12) and became uncovered in his tent.

You need to take heed in anything you do, don't say in your heart "I work for my money I can do what I like with my money and myself." You are not the owner of yourself neither your money.

Excess in everything is bad and if care is not taken it will turn to lasciviousness. Whatever you are going to do, eating or drinking do all for the glory of God (1 Corinthians 10: 31) Don't use the Word of God to suit yourself.

Let us look at the power of God and frailty of man. The man Noah walked uprightly before God, he was found faithful among all men on the face of the earth. He got drunk and uncovered himself in his tent. Proverbs 20:1 says *"wine is a mocker strong drink is a brawler and who ever led astray by it is not wise."*

No matter who we are in the hands of the Lord, let us take heed less we fall into temptation, the book of Ephesians 5:18 says and do not be drunk with wine in which is dissipation but be filled with the spirit of God. We have to maintain our spiritual life. We need to discipline ourselves not only wine but anything that befits the name of our master.

Whatever you are struggling with, give it to Jesus he will help you out that is why he came. Noah fell asleep and disaster entered his house. His son Ham, father of Canaan entered his room and saw his nakedness. He told his brother and he was sensible enough to cover their father's nakedness. What Ham did brought a curse upon his life (Genesis 23: 25). Noah's lack of control caused a problem in his household. Obedience is a long-term commitment. A man may be faithful but his sinful nature needs to be dealt with. We need to be filled with the spirit of God. There is no way we can make it on our own that is why Jesus was sent (John 14:17). Ham's descendant were the first to be cursed in the Bible.

We can see that Canaanites did become slaves of Shem his brother, the father of Hebrews, during Israel's monarchy. God enlarged Japheth. God's incorporation of gentiles awaited the new covenant. The family of Noah now divided into the uttermost part of the earth after the flood (Genesis 10:33).

We are now ruling under the covenant of God. There is a time for everything, seed time and harvest time, cold and heat God created the first thing with the ability to grow and multiply. Let this sink into your heart today, your life begins by the principle of seed and harvest time, there is time for everything. Once you know this, you will know how to wait on the Lord without grumbling and complaining.

(Ecclesiastes 3:1) To everything there is season. A time to every purpose under heaven. A time to be born and a time to die. A time to plant and a time to pluck up what is planted. For each thing has it's proper time or cycle. Make sure your life is fruitful and multiply in all that you do. God has spoken and it will come to pass if you believe in Him. He is able to do all that He has said. He says *"every word that proceeded from my mouth will not come back to me without doing what l send it to do."*

The choice is yours. If you believe, you will eat the best in God.

Terah was the father of Abraham, during this time Abraham's people refused to serve God. They ignored him and continued sinning, but a handful of them genuinely followed the Lord. Out of them was Abram's father, we read that he left his town with his children from Ur of the Chaldeans to the land of Canaan and they came to Haran and dwelt thus.

Genesis 11:31-32 says and Terah took his son Abram and his grandson Lot the son of Haran and his daughter in-law Sarah, his son Abram's wife, and they went out with them to Ur of the Chaldeans to go to the land of Canaan, and Terah died in Haran. God was with Abram and the intent of God was to save his people through Abram.

I want to let you know that the grace of God is for everybody. God is not looking for a complete perfect man and woman. What he needs is your availability. Once you fear him and make yourself available He will work on you through His power.

God made a covenant with Abram to make him the father of many nations.

God reveals his truth and beauty to the world through redeemed mankind. Abraham was called out by God when he was 75 years old. God was just looking for one man to stand in the gap for his people.

GOD now bound himself to Abraham in Genesis 12:1-3, God called him out and he went and he was counted for him to be righteous because he obeyed God's voice. Now the Lord had said to Abram *"get out of your country from your family and from your father's house to the land that l will show you. I will make you a great nation, l will bless you and make your name great, and you shall be a blessing. I will bless those who bless you, and I will curse those who curse you, and in you all the families of the earth shall be blessed."*

God separated Abraham from his father's house in order to make him and his descendants the messianic nation which you and I are in (Galatians 3:13-14). Through the death of our Lord Jesus on the cross he did for us what we could not do for ourselves. His work not ours removed the curse and the blessing of Abraham become ours. By faith we received all the benefits provided by his death including justification, spiritual blessing, emotionally, physically and materially.

God will bless those who bless you and curse those who curse you, isn't God good and gracious? With all the blessings of God Abraham was without a child his wife was barren but still faithful to God, he went back to God and made his request known to God.

God saw his heart and visited him again to renew his covenant and comforted him by his Word (Genesis 15:1-5) God told him not to be afraid that He, God, is his shield. After these things the Word of the Lord came to Abraham in a vision saying, *"do not be afraid Abraham. I am your shield your exceedingly great reward."* But Abram said, *"look you have given me no offspring, indeed one born in my house is my heir." Though the culture permitted a senior slave to become heir of a childless man, and behold, the word of the Lord came to him, saying, this one shall not be your heir, but one who will be your heir, will come out of your own body shall be your heir."* Then he brought him outside and said, *"look now forward heaven, and count the stars if you are able to number them,"* and he said to him *"so shall your descendant be."*

And Abram believed what the Lord said and God was very pleased with Abram because of his faith in him. This moved God and set a stage for the covenant. Only your faith in the finished work on Calvary can move God, without that you can not please Him. The covenant that God made was established in the blood.

Genesis 15:7-10 says "I am the Lord who brought you out of Ur of Chaldeans, to give you this land to inherit it. And he said "Lord God, how shall I know that I will inherit it.

So He said to him, "Bring me a three years old heifer, a three year old female goat, a three year old ram, a turtledove, and a young pigeon." Then he brought all these to him and cut them in two, down the middle, and placed each piece opposite the other; Abram put down the goat and the turtle dove, young pigeon by sacrifice the covenant, parties passed between the halves indicating that they were bound together in the blood.

God came down and passed between those pieces and made himself so low for mankind. Instead of Abram speaking, God spoke and the Lord made promises to

Abraham. He voluntarily made himself lower than man for the establishment of the covenant. God took the oath of loyalty.

God promised Abram and bound Himself with him saying if I break this bound let me be like these pieces. God's love extends to everybody. He has made provision for us all through His Son . This covenant is for you and me. He has promised not to leave you for He will keep you with everlasting love. Compare the love of God to human love. Man will love you when you are good to them, but as soon as you offend one you are hated. No man can love you the way God loves you. Unconditional love is not because you are good but the mercy of God.

The Bible says "greater love has no one than this than to lay down one's life for his friends." Who can measure this love? Christ gave his glory, comforts, joys, and adoration of heaven to carry the sin of the sinners. God is a good God.

The promise that God had for Abraham and his wife was to give them a child. But, they took the law onto their hands because of her barrenness. She now gave Hagar her maidservant to her husband in substitution for the promise of God. When the Word of God says in (Isaiah 55: 8-9&11) *"For my thought are completely different from yours says the Lord and my ways are far beyond any thing you could imagine. For just as the heavens are higher than the earth, so are my ways higher than your ways and my thoughts higher than your thoughts. It is the same with my word. I send it out, it always produces fruit, it will accomplish all I want it to and it will prosper everywhere I send it."*

God's Word is never barren. The power of God is in His word. Do not give up on the promise of God in your life. A thousand years is a night before God. He will come. Obey Him and you will be at peace in every area of your life.

Abraham and Sarah could not wait for the promise of God. That's what we are facing today. Hagar gave birth to Ishmael which they all thought to be their joy but it turned out against them. This was no fault of the boy for he knew no sin. Indeed God's blessing was upon Ishmael. God still brought something good out of Ishmael's life.

He was Abraham's descendant. He was with Abraham when God introduced the covenant of circumcision. The act of circumcision symbolised the covenant and the establishment of Abraham and his descendant. The covenant stood as a hope in the future for the people of Israel. This is how Ishmael was traced as the father of Arabia's modern day. God named the maidservant 's son because of His favour upon all. He always extends His love to you. He knows your affliction but you have to allow Him.

God created Abraham and his family including Ishmael, to serve and worship Him. Though Abraham had to send the maidservant and her son away as it was directed, for he was not the promised son. All their efforts to help God only brought problems to their family. We don't need to help God, just trust in Him (Galatians 4:24).

As God wanted Abraham and his people to love and serve Him alone, so also He wants you to love and serve Him. No matter where you find yourself in the world, the reason of your essence is to serve the Lord, for God is jealous for His people. He doesn't want you to serve any other god except Him.

Exodus 20:3-5 says *"you shall have no other gods before me. You shall not make for yourself a calf of image any likeness of anything that is in heaven above, or that is in the earth beneath, or that is in the water under the earth; you shall not bow down to them nor serve them. For I, the Lord your God, am a jealous God."*

His character demands faithfulness and loyalty. When we worship the true God we demonstrate loyalty to Him who is seated on the throne. We show Him that we love him and that we acknowledge His existence. No human effort could represent God adequately. He is the "I am that I am." He says I forbid you creating any graven image either literally or conceptually.

Get rid of anything that wants to stand between you and God. Let God be the centre of your life and you will see His mighty hand in your life. Ishmael was born to serve God. He could not be blamed for the wrong steps taken by Abraham and Sarah. He was born and grew up in a difficult atmosphere especially when his father sent him out. Though God's Word says his hand will be upon his brother, Isaac, he was still blessed and favoured by God, showing the mercy of God.

But his mother took him out and showed him another god. A god having mouth but cannot speak, eyes but cannot see. She took a wife for him in the "land of empty" which means the world. This opened his eyes to see what he should not see and serve gods he should not serve. This was a man that had the covenant of circumcision with God and his father Abraham. Circumcision was instituted by God as a sign forever. It was a sign of obedience. A symbol of cutting off the life of sin. Once you circumcise there is no turning back.

Genesis 17:4-24 & Luke 9: 62 says Jesus said to them "one having put his hand to the plow, and looking back, is not fit for the kingdom of God. Ishmael was identified as Jewish (1 Chronicles 1:28). The Bible called him the son of Abraham. A covenant man mixed with unbelievers and the wind of the world blew him away and he lost sight to worship the true God.

This takes me to the book of Genesis 34:1-15 when Jacob's daughter Dinah was found spoiled by shechem son of Hamor the hivith. Jacob and the whole family was displeased, even God was not happy about it. Hamor made every attempt for Shechem to marry Dinah but they refused to allow him be part of them because they were uncircumcised people. I am saying this to let you know the importance of circumcision among God's people.

Where we trace the twelve princes of Ishmael that joined hands and bowed down to other gods, it is time for every tongue and tribe to come home to the true God which is the right way. Jesus has paid the price for all the debt through the deal that was done through His blood. It has repaired every thing that was spoiled between us and God the father.

For God demonstrate his own love toward us, that while we were yet sinners Christ died for us much more then, having now been justified by his blood we shall be saved from the wrath of God through him.

Romans 5: 8-9 (NIV)

The blood of Jesus established that all are unrighteous and therefore deserved judgement. For without the shedding of the blood there is no remission of sin. The Bible says all of us, all means all. No not one that does good without Christ Jesus in his or her life.

The Bible says in Genesis 6:5 *"then the Lord saw the wickedness of man was great in the earth; and that every intent of thoughts of his heart was only evil continually."* Tell me how you are going to make it without the Redeemer in your life. I am not talking about the wealth of this world. I am talking about the real plan of God in your life. To be fulfiled you need to come to Him. You are absolutely in need of restoration in your life. What will it profit a man to gain the whole world and lose his or her soul. Believe in the blood, for the love of God has reached out beyond the the satisfaction of justice to establish the bond of fellowship in the blood of His Son Jesus Christ. Faith and obedience in the blood not only brings our deliverance from the wrath of God, but is also the means of victorious living, through participation in His life.

This shows that the blood of Jesus Christ deals with the legal separation from God. He reconciles us to Him. Faith and obedience in the name of Jesus gives us divine life and provision.

For our continual triumph over sin, the blood is enough for us. Not by human work that any one should boast. Just trust in the blood He will do you good. God's love for you and me irrevocable and unconditional. You are the image of God. You are the descendant of Abraham God's friend. Remember He made you to be what you are today. Why do you say "there is no God" or that He is too big or holy to come down in the likeness of his son to save? Is He not the same God that came down in the likeness of an angel to Hagar, mother of Ishmael, to comfort her and provide for her need when there was no water to drink.

You need Him in your life more than gold or silver . He loves you the way you are. He will save you and give you everlasting joy. Can we blame Ishmael or God for what happened? Absolutely not. Not Ishmael neither God, not even the two mothers. All is for the glory of God. It is for a purpose don't separate yourself from God.

I want you to realise this: human frailty spoilt the whole earth. Man will be man, God will be God. Man is not perfect neither responsible or reliable or stable but God is not like man. He is perfect reliable, responsible, and stable. If you can see Him as all in all it will open you to your need in God at all time.

It was through human searching for knowledge they hide under another way of serving God. (Ecclesiastes:7-29 says *"Truly, this only I have found: that God made man upright, but they have sought out many schemes."*

The Lord warns and encourages us to trust in Him and not lean on our own understanding: even in all our ways we should acknowledge Him. You must be fully aware that he exists and He will direct your paths. You need to come out from Adam and give your life to Jesus, He will save you. Christianity is not a religion but a personal relationship with God through His Son. No one can save you. Your good doing can do you nothing. Not the blood covenant between you and any man can save you but the blood of Jesus. He is the lamb that was slain for the sin of the world.

As I said your goodness cannot save you from the wrath of God but faith in Jesus Christ the hope of glory. The blood of Jesus Christ has been shed for the whole world. Remember there is no repentance in the grave. Jesus Christ is the only way to the Father, the owner of the whole world, the "I am that I am." This was said to Moses when God sent him to his people in Egypt for they had many gods in Egypt. The name "I am that I am" described His eternal power and unchangeable character. God's nature is stable and trust worthy. His name in Hebrew translated as Yahweh is derived from "I am" He reminded Moses of His promises to Abraham, isaac and Jacob. He used the "I am" to show His stability. Whatever He says will surely come to pass.

He sent His Son to redeem mankind. Salvation is for everyone. You don't need to make another god for yourself. You need to come out of the world that has nothing to offer you. The world and everything in it will melt away. The people of Egypt and all mankind were created to serve God for the blood of Jesus is shed for you and the whole world.

John 3:16 says *"For God so loved the world that he gave his only begotten son, that whoever believes in Him should not perish but have everlasting life."* Our lives are hid in the name of Jesus Christ, without him you are missing the mark, the purpose of God for your life. Will you be ready when Jesus Christ comes? Can he welcome you into His rest?

CHAPTER 3

LIFE IN CHRIST JESUS THE GOOD SHEPHERD

I am the good shepherd. The good shepherd lays down his life for the sheep.

John 10:11 (NIV)

For by Him all things were created that are in heaven and invisible, whether thrones or dominions or principalities or powers all things were created through Him and for Him. And he is before all things. And in Him all things consist.

Colossians 1: 16; 17 (NKJV)

Consist means to hold or stand in oneness. God is not only the Creator of the world but He is also the Sustainer, in Him everything is held together, protected and prevented from disintegrating into chaos. Therefore none of us is independent of Him. We are all His servants who must daily trust in Him A shepherd means herdsman, sheep herder and one who tends flocks. King David says the Lord is my shepherd I shall not want. Who is your shepherd? Your wealth or your position in society? Ecclesiastes 1:2 says "vanity of vanities, all is vanity."

That means whatever or whoever we are, without Him in our lives we are nothing. If we live, we live to the Lord; and if we die; we die to the Lord. Therefore whether we live or die, we are the Lord's. You can see the reason why we need Him.

He loves you and laid down His life for us. He promises you abundant life, super abundance, excessive, more than enough, profuse, extraordinary above the ordinary, more than sufficiency. This is the life that God desires for you. Sow the seed of faith as you give your total life to God for the thief of your soul comes to steal, kill and to destroy but Jesus the good shepherd has come to give you life in abundance.

God of Abundance

He promises you real possibility of health for your total being-body mind and emotions including prosperity. Do not be deceived by the voice of the devil that always tells you that you don't need God or if you confess Him as your Lord and Saviour you can still do fornication, envy, slanderer, adultery, uncleanness, drunkenness, revelries, jealousy, sorcery, hatred and so on. I am telling you whosoever practice these will not enter the kingdom of God. Revelation 21:27 says there is no uncleanness that will enter therein. If we say we are saved and still wallow in sin , we disobey God. And for those that are yet to be saved, you are out of God's will for your life. It is time for you to come to the owner of your life. He loves you. He alone can help you. This is the reason why our Saviour came.

Let no one deceive you with empty words for because of this the wrath of God comes upon the sons of disobedience.

Therefore do not be partakers with them for you were once in darkness but you are now light in the world; now walk as children of light for life has being given to us through our Lord Jesus.

Blessed be the God and father of our Lord Jesus christ who according to his abundant mercy has begotten us again to a living hope through the resurrection of Jesus christ from the died.

I Peter 1:3 (NKJV)

If you are yet to accept Jesus as your Lord and saviour please do so. As I said earlier on, satan is the ruler of this world. The line is clearly drawn but God's goodness has made provision for our life that whosoever believes in Him shall not perish but have eternal life. Eternal life is God's life embodied in Christ to all believers as a guarantee that they will live forever where there is no death, sickness, or sin neither enemy.

This life is just an introduction to eternity. If you can say "yes" to Jesus you settle for your everlasting home.

The enemy wants you to suffer loss. He wants to rob you off from God's blessing, oppress your bodies through diseases and accident, loneliness, joblessness, bareness and destroy everything you love .

God's desire is to bless you, heal and make you whole Jeremiah 29:11 says "for I know the thoughts I think toward you, says the Lord thoughts of peace and not of evil to give you future and hope." His word never fails. He wants you to be happy and prosper. His plan for us is to be enriched and have a prosperous life and have dominion even in abundance Amen.

Jesus came to declare what the intent of the father was and the intent of the devil. The intent of the devil is to hinder the promise of God for mankind. But to God be the glory, through His only begotten Son we have received eternal life. He also came to deliver mankind from death by His resurrection from the dead and to open a new dimension of life for us so that all things in Him are new.

JESUS THE WAY TO THE FATHER

I am the way the truth and the life. No one comes to the father except through Me.

John 14:6 (NKJV)

He is the truth about God and the very life of God. He reveals the glory of God to us. There is no other way to communicate to the father. He is the one that bridges the gap between man and God. He has made himself a sacrifice once and for all for you and me. He has shed his blood for us that we be not condemned but Redeemed.

God did not send His son into the world to condemn the world but that the world through him might be saved. He who believes in him is not condemned but he who does not believe is condemned already because he did not believe in the name of the only begotten son of God

And this is the condemnation that the light has come into the world and that men loved darkness rather than light. Because their deeds were evil.

John 3:19

You need to be born again. Jesus says "repent for the kingdom of God is at hand." A kingdom is a place where a king rules. The kingdom of God is where God reigns over the lives of His subjects. The kingdom of God is not visible because God is not visible. It is a spiritual kingdom. It is eternal. Where are you going to spend your eternity?

For the heavens will pass away with a great noise, and the elements will melt with fervent heat; both the earth and works that are in it will be burned up. See this world will end one day. Salvation is free. Receive Him and live and reign with Him where there will be one government ruling. Religion cannot save you. Going to church and being born in the church without Jesus is meaningless. What you need to do is just give Him your life and be born of God's nature. Confess Him as your Lord and Saviour. Romans 10:10 says that "if you confess with your mouth the Lord Jesus and believe in your heart that God raised Him from the dead you will be saved."

For with the heart one believes unto righteousness and with the mouth confession is made unto salvation. After the confession you are saved, you born of the Word of God and partakers of the divine nature of God. You are now a new creature, old things have passed away in your life.

The devil can not mess you up again, for greater is He that is in you than he that is in the world. You have been redeemed and your evil conscience has been washed away by the blood of Jesus. You are no longer living by your own but by the Holy Spirit, a person like Jesus with whom you are sealed till the day of our Lord's return. Surrender to Him and your life will not be the same again. Taste and see that the Lord is good.

STEPS TO TAKE AFTER BEING BORN AGAIN

Now you are born again, a new person in God, the first thing you experience in your life is the peace of God. Jesus said in His word "peace I leave with you, my peace I give to you not as the world gives." I personally experienced it when I gave my life to Jesus. He even changed my views and from the worries of life. Not that I don't have ups and downs, but through the grace of God I always overcome. Once you are in the Lord victory is yours in Jesus name Amen.

Secondly you will hate sin and love to do well because of the new nature and through the help of the Holy Spirit. Proverbs 20:27 says *"the spirit of man is the lamp of the Lord."* The spirit of God relates with our inner man.

The inner man is the light that guides us. That is why we need to renew our minds with the Word of God. For we war not with flesh and blood but against principalities and powers against the rulers of this darkness of this age. Apostle Paul says in 2 Corinthians 10:4 *"for the weapons of our warfare are not carnal, not what we can see, but are mighty of God for pulling down strongholds. Casting down arguments and every high thing that exalts itself against the knowledge of God."* We need the power of God to pull down everything opposing the knowledge of God in our life especially our mind-set, Pride, arrogant rebellious attitudes bringing them to the obedience of Christ.

Though we are saved, our flesh still wars against the spirit. When we got saved it was our spirit that got saved. We are Spirit, soul, and body. God is Spirit. His Spirit connects our spirit with His word. The soul is what we need to renew with the Word of God. To correct our daily lives we need to die to flesh cause the flesh is the enemy of God for it can not please Him.

> **for those who live according to the flesh set their mind on the things of the flesh, but those who live according to the spirit the things of the spirit. For to be carnally minded is death, but to be Spiritually minded is life and peace.**
>
> **Romans 8:5 (NKJV)**

We can see in this passage the carnal mind is enmity against God. It cannot be subject to the things of God. From here you can see why we need to feed our mind day by day. God told Joshua not to let the word depart from him to live a prosperous life. What about you? You and I need it.

Let the Word of God be the mirror of your life that reflects the glory of God. Let it be water that washes you everyday of your life. When satan tempted our Lord Jesus He responded with the word. He knew the power that is in the Word of God.

> For the Word of God is living and powerful, and sharper than any two-edged sword, piercing even to the division of soul and Spirit, and joint and marrow, and is a discerner of the thoughts and intents of the heart, and there is no creature hidden from His sight. But all things are naked and open to the eyes of Him to whom we must give account.
>
> Hebrews 4:12 (NKJV)

At this point you might be thinking on the journey and how it will be. but don't worry. The Holy Spirit will help you and me in the journey we have embarked upon. It is not a one day journey but the Holy Spirit helps us along the process. John 16. 8 tells about the work of the Holy Spirit. He is a Helper, Standby, Strength, Comforter, Intercessor, Advocate and Counsellor. He is the Attorney who always appears in every place for us. The fact that you are led by the spirit of God you are a son or daughter of God. You are not on your own.

Romans 14:7-8 says For none of us lives to himself. Therefore, whether we live or die we are the Lord's. Therefore separate yourself from the world. Romans 12:1-2 says *"do not be conformed to this world, but be transformed by the renewing of your mind."* Set yourself aside. Make yourself a living sacrifice, holy acceptable for this is your reasonable service to the Lord. Don't give yourself to the worldly things.

HOW WOULD I KNOW THAT AM SAVED?

This question affected me so much when I was first saved. I still had it in mind that I was not saved. Each time a preacher made an altar call I would come out and confess Jesus again. But to God be the glory, Romans 10:11 became alive to me and changed my life. Even if I sin against the Holy Spirit what I do is to confess. I confess my sin according to 1 John 1:9, re-dedicate my life again to Jesus and start enjoying the grace that God has given to me through His Son Jesus Christ. I am not saying to you that sin is good or that you should go on sinning.

We cannot be in sin and ask for the grace of God to abound, of course not. That is why we need Jesus everyday of our lives. Brother and sister, once you believe and confess with your mouth and are baptised, you are saved. Don't doubt your salvation. Don't try to work things out. The Holy Spirit will help you.

Jesus is aware of our incompleteness and our weakness that is why He gave us the Holy Spirit; a Person like him. He is the Person that works in the Creation. The same Person that walked with our Lord Jesus Christ when He was here on earth for 33 years is the same One with us now in all things we do.

Jesus said to His disciples before His death that if He did not go away, the Comforter would not come. It was better for Him to go for the fulfilment of the Word of God.

> But now I am going away to the one who sent me, and none of you has asked me where I am going. Instead you are very sad. But it is actually best for you that I go away. Because if I don't, the Counsellor won't come. If I go away He will come because I will send Him to you. And when He comes He will convict the world of sin and of righteousness and of judgment.
>
> John 16:5-8

He has given us all that we have. The Spirit himself bear witness with our Spirit that we are the children of God and joint heirs with Christ. If we indeed we suffer, we suffer with Him that that we may also be glorified together with Him.

The Spirit will help us to maintain what Christ has done for us. God has made everything for us to enjoy. You can come to Him for the curtain of the temple has been torn from the top to the bottom to give you free access to Him.

You can come with boldness to God. For now there is no condemnation to those who are in Christ Jesus, who do not walk according to the flesh but according to the Spirit. He has used his blood to cleanse your conscience. Submit now to your Master the overseer of your soul.

Lay aside every weight and sin which easily ensnares you and look unto Him. Depend on Him. God loves us with an everlasting love. He is faithful and not a man that He should lie nor a son of man that he should repent.

His Word is true so let us daily lay aside our daily desires to follow Him. Putting all our energy and resources at his disposal and trusting Him we should joyfully give ourselves as a living sacrifice for His service. God's love and his mercies must move us to please Him.

No man must think too much of himself. satan exalts himself above God. He was cast down from heaven and was demoted, stripped off and rendered powerless because of you and me. Meditate on the death and the resurrection of our Lord Jesus Christ. He will do you well, not by power but by the Spirit of God Amen.

for the grace of God that brings salvation has appeared to all men..

Titus 2:11 (NKJV)

Look at that to "ALL MEN" young and old! What you need to do is to say "no" to ungodliness and worldly passions and to live self-controlled, upright and godly in this present age.

CHAPTER 4

THE FEARFULNESS OF
GOD'S JUDGEMENT.

And behold I am coming quickly and my reward is with me to give to every one according to his work.

Revelation 22:12 (NKJV)

Behold He is coming with clouds and every eye will see Him. Even they who pierced Him and all the tribes of the earth will mourn. Because of Him even so Amen.

Revelation 1:7 (NKJV)

The word Amen confirms His coming as a king and Judge. He will judge the world accordingly whether good or bad. Matthew 24:3-14 has given us clarity of the signs of His coming; pestilence, nation against nation, hearing of wars and rumours of wars and the preaching of the gospel in all nations. Many of these are fulfiled already and many more are to come. But he who endures to the end shall be saved, but whosoever does not believe shall be condemned. Which side are you on? Be prepared for there is going to be a great tribulation.

But the true believer will not be deceived.

"for then there will be great tribulation, such as has not been since the beginning of the world until this time, no, nor ever shall be." **And unless those days were shortened no flesh would be saved ; but for the elects sake those days will be shortened**

Then if anyone says to you look here is the Christ or there; do not believe it. For false Christ and false prophets will rise and show great signs and wonders to deceive, if possible even the elect, see I have told you before hand. Therefore if they say to you look He is in the desert do not go out or look, or He is in the inner rooms; do not believe it for as the lightning comes from the east and flashes to the west so also will the coming of the son of Man will be.

Matthew 24:21-28 (NKJV)

It is not going to be hidden at all you will see it with your eyes. The teaching of Jesus should create a Spirit of watchfulness among His followers As a church we need to wake up from our slumber and steadfastly trust Christ. For everything that can be shaken will be shaken. Please hold your faith in Christ persecution will come. If care is not taken the so called elect will find it difficult to be loyal to the call of God in there lives. I want us to believe one thing; God is in control of even the length of the persecutions. He will not leave or forget His people.

He who called us is faithful. He will do it. But for those who would postpone their faith in Christ till tomorrow, it may be too late. This is the time of God's favour.

in an acceptable time I have heard you and in the day of
salvation I have helped you. Behold now is the day of salvation.

2 Corinthians 6:2 (NKJV)

The Greek word is "chairs" and means an appointed
time or season rather than a certain length of time. The
right time to receive God's grace is now. The grace will
cease, therefore as the Holy Spirit says today if you will
hear His voice do not harden your hearts as the day of
trial in the wilderness. The Holy Spirit used the failure
of the Israelites in the wilderness as an example. I want
to let you know the spirit of disobedience resulted in
God's wrath. Beware lest you fall into the trap of the
enemy.

and to give you who are troubled rest with us when the
Lord Jesus is revealed from heaven with his mighty angels
in flaming fire taking vengeance on those who do not obey
the gospel of our Lord Jesus Christ. These shall be
punished with everlasting destruction from the glory of
His power.

2 Thessalonians 1:7-9 (NKJV)

The wicked will be banished from the Lord's presence but the true believer will be with our Lord in his
glory. Jesus is coming to Judge the whole earth, what
will be your faith?

All what is written in the Bible are examples and they
were written for our admonition upon whom the ends
of the ages have come. We need to understand that we

are now living in an overlap between the former and the new creation. Let us give all to God

If you are a Christian playing with sin, repent and forsake them and God will have mercy upon you for He has no pleasure in the death of the wicked. He has nothing to gain in that . That is why He sent His Son to die for our sin.

> **As I live, says the Lord God, I have no pleasure in the death of the wicked, but that the wicked turn from his way and live. Turn, turn from evil way; for why should you die O house of israel.**
>
> **Ezekiel 33:11-19 (NKJV)**

You may say "I am not an Israelite. This is not talking to me." I want to let you know, once you make up your mind to follow Jesus as your Lord and your saviour you are joint heir of Abraham father of faith. All the word Written in the Bible is for you and if you can take the word and allow the Holy Spirit to minister to you it shall be well with you. You are a spiritual Israelite. Think about this passage in the Bible Roman 11:21 *"if God did not spare the natural branches He may not spare you either."*

He has placed before us curses and blessing. It is a matter of choice and it is better to choose life. If you choose life you will live, if not you will be condemned. The Bible exhorts, Do not harden your heart. He who overcomes will inherit the kingdom of the Father where God will wipe all tears away. Please do not let this word become veiled to your face.

Behold His Glory and live. This is the delight to those that love His word.

> but we have renounced the hidden things of shame not walking in craftiness nor handling the Word of God deceitfully. But by manifestation of the truth commending ourselves to Every man's conscience in the sight of God. But if our gospel is veiled, it is veiled to those who are perishing whose minds the god of this age has blinded who do not believe lest the light of the gospel of glory of Christ who is the image of God should shine on them.
>
> 2 Corinthians 4:2-4 (NKJV)

Do not fix your eyes on what you see now. What you see now is temporary but what you do not see is eternal Amen (2 Corinthians 4:18). Allow the mystery to be known to you. Open up for the coming King. Come out from your unbelief. Join the saints so that you do not see corruption. If not the womb that gave birth to you will forget you talk less of God. Your memories will not be remembered as if you were never born at all (Job 24:19-20).

Do not wait for any sign like Gideon before you believe God. There is potential in you. Gideon demanded a sign and it was given him by a loving God for he knows our weakness. But I want to let you know that you have a better covenant than him today. The people of Israel also asked for signs from Jesus before they could believe.

Jesus said to them that the only sign they would be

given was the sign of Jonah who was in the belly of the fish for three days and three nights (Matthew 12:38-41) Judges 7:36-40). You don't need a sign, just believe Jesus as your Lord and saviour and you will be saved. Jesus said to Thomas; " *because you see me you have believed. Blessed are those who have not seen me and yet believe.*" God said to Moses that He will hide his face for the Israelite faithlessness in Him (Deuteronomy 32:20)And He said ; "*I will hide my face from them. I will see what their end will be for they are a perverse generation. Children in whom is no faith.*"

Jesus has done all on the cross once and for all. Without the cross there will be no grace and mercy. He is the son of God seeking those that was lost. He is the bridegroom and we are the bride. He is coming to marry those that believe in His name. The Spirit of God and the bride says "come Lord Jesus" (Revelation 20:10).

It is the final harvest and He is coming to pour His judgement and wrath upon the devil and restore the kingdom of God back to the rightful place. A new Heaven new Earth where there will be no death, sorrow nor sickness but peace. A place where wild animals will live in peace with domestic animals (Isaiah 11:6-9). Jesus Christ will reign as king and the kingdom will be established on earth. There will be one government under the leadership of our Lord Jesus Christ.

HELL AND HADES

> And if your hand cause you to sin pluck it out, it is better for you to enter the kingdom of God with one eye rather than having two eyes to be cast into hell fire where their worm does not die. And the fire is not quenched.
>
> **Mark 9:47-48 (NKJV)**

It is a place of worms and maggots, fire and problem. It is a place of perpetual burning but is not meant for you and me. Hell is for the devil and for the fake prophet. Why can't you experience the present pain and deny yourself the pleasure of this world that will end one day, than eternal torments.

The world and all the pleasure in it will pass away including your enjoyment here on earth, position, wealth and degree. Without Jesus what will it profit a man or a woman to gain the world and pleasure and lose his or her soul. Please ponder on this in your heart. The Bible says in Ecclesiastes 1:1 " *'meaningless! meaningless!'says the teacher. 'Utterly meaningless! Everything is meaningless."*

This word came from inspiration that God gave to king Solomon the son of king David who had everything (wisdom, power, honour, reputation, riches, God's favour). He discussed the ultimate emptiness of all the world has to give.

He is telling the whole world to learn not to have confidence in their own efforts, abilities, and righteousness but in God the only reason for living. Think about the life of this king.

He says "I thought in my heart, 'come now, I will test you with pleasure to find out what is good.' But that also proved to be meaningless. 'Laughter,' I said, is foolish. And what does pleasure accomplish? I tried cheering myself with wine and embracing folly-my mind still guiding me with wisdom. The wisdom he is talking about here is human knowledge that can be disastrous without God's guidance. He even undertook great projects, built houses for himself, planted vineyards, made gardens and parks and planted all kinds of fruit trees in them. He made reservoirs to water groves of flourishing trees. He even bought male and female slaves. He says to himself that "I denied myself nothing my eyes desired; I refused my heart no pleasure.

My heart took delight in all my work and this was the reward for all my labour yet when I surveyed all that my hands had toiled to achieve, everything was meaningless, a chasing after the wind. Nothing was gained under the sun. Solomon himself summarised all his attempts to find life's meaning as chasing after wind. We know as the wind passes we can't catch hold of it or keep it in all our accomplishments.

King Solomon wrote in the book of psalm 127: 1 *"Unless the Lord builds the house, the builders labour in vain. Unless the Lord watches the city, the watchmen stand guard in vain."* As you examine your goals in life what is your starting point? Without God as your foundation all you are living for is meaningless. We must not build our lives on perishable pursuits but on the solid foundation of God.

We can learn a lot in this king's life. He was chosen by God and followed God's ordinances even in his early age. After being ordained by his father for the fulfilment of the Word of God, Solomon's desire was to please God. When asked by God what he required from Him, Solomon did not ask for money nor power but wisdom that would enable him to look after the people of God. He recognised his incompetence and surrendered all to God. The Lord was very pleased and blessed him not only with wisdom but with such wealth that no one on earth has attained to this day. But after eating and making merry in his heart he messed up and started doing what pleased him and not what pleased God who chose him as king.

It was a sad ending (????Kings 2:1-28) [?????Kings 9:1-28] Solomon went against not only his father's last words but also God's direct commands. His action reminds us how easy it is to know what is right and yet fail to do it. The book of James says anyone then who knows the good he ought to do and doesn't do it, sins. You see where this noble king missed it. We can categorise his way of life into two ways for anyone not to have any excuses

1. If you are running after wealth without the giver of life, your wealth will not give you any reason to give your life to Jesus Christ. He is telling you today to give him your heart. *"My son give me thine heart"* (Proverbs 23:26) is His urgent request to you. 1 Timothy 6:7-10 says *"After all, we didn't bring anything with us when we came into the world, and we certainly cannot carry anything with us when we die. If we have enough food and clothing,* *let us be content. But people who long to be rich fall into temptation and are trapped by many foolish and harmful desires that plunge them into ruin and destruction. For the love of money is at the root of all kinds of evil. And some people craving money, have wandered from the faith and pierced themselves with many sorrows."* Will you allow God to have His way with you? He will help you to live a victorious life.

2. You that started with Christ Jesus with all his spiritual and physical blessing and then started compromising had better stop. Learn from other's mistakes. Remember there is no where you can hide or go in the face of the earth that He will not find you out. Your sin will surely find you out. Return back to your Creator. What He needs from you is "sorry." He will restore your soul and His grace will be multiply in your life. Let the love of God motivate your life by obeying His word.

Judgement of God

As I said earlier on, God has given men to die once after that Judgement. The place hell is an outer darkness where you will be lonely and separated from God, man, all your riches, your lovely friends, food, power, all your knowledge, wisdom and beautiful houses will be left behind. Think of this: those who chose hell will be put into inky blackness of eternity with no wife or husband nor children to talk to again. There will be no second chance.

There was a story about the rich man and a man named Lazarus. There is nothing bad in having wealth. Wealth with Christ will do you good. With Christ you will even enjoy your wealth here on earth. Being poor is not a passport to heaven. One's destiny depends upon your relationship with God (Luke 12:15). The choice is yours.

It is better you chose life according to the Word of God (Deuteronomy 30:19). I have set before you life and death ,blessing and cursing, therefore choose life. God does not want anybody to perish but to repent and live. He has no hand in destroying people. It is we people that forget where we came from and start living a life that pleases us when the Bible says there is a way that pleases man but the end is death.

The rich man died and went to hell. The Bible calls it Hades: a place of eternal punishment. But the poor man died and went to heaven. (Luke 16:19-31) says "there was a certain rich man who was clothed in purple and fine linen and fared sumptuously everyday. But there was a certain beggar named Lazarus full of sores who was laid at his gate desiring to be fed with the crumbs which fell from the rich man's table.

Moreover the dogs came and licked his sores so it was that the beggar died and was carried by the angels to Abraham's bosom (A place of honour in paradise). The rich man also died and was buried. With all his wealth he still died (vanity upon vanity, all is vanity! What a pity) and being in torment in Hades he lifted up his eyes and saw Abraham afar off and Lazarus in his bosom." Think about this word "afar off."

There will be a gap between Hades and heaven. A place where mother cannot help or children nor husband or wife. Today, as you are reading this book, is the day of salvation. Tomorrow may be too late. Please repent for the kingdom of God is at hand.

Read on... "then the rich man cried and said 'father Abraham have mercy on me and send Lazarus that he may put the tip of his finger in the water and cool my tongue for I am tormented in this flame. " He still had the picture of Lazarus a poor man with sores in his leg licked by dogs and not seeing him as a glorious person (Pride).. 'send Lazarus' "but Abraham said 'son remember that your lifetime you received your good things and likewise Lazarus evil things but now he is comforted and you are tormented and beside all this, between us and you there is a great gulf. So that those who want to pass from there to us cannot.

'Wealth is good as I said but without God it is useless.' Jesus is calling the rich and the poor to repent. No woman or man must live a self centred life but rather be under the Lordship of Jesus Christ . He has made himself to be poor for you and me to be rich. Check your life and yield your heart to find God and he will draw near unto you.

> "For whoever finds me finds life and obtains favour from the Lord. But he who sins against me wrongs his own soul! All those who hate me love death. What will it profit a man gaining the whole world and lose his soul."
>
> **Proverbs 8:35-36 (NKJV)**

A man cannot redeem his soul with money or any sacrifice other than the blood of Jesus that was shed for the remission of our sins. Mankind was not made for hell but whoever chooses to reject God through His Son Jesus Christ one day will end his or her journeying in eternal punishment.

God extends His love to all through the death and the resurrection of Jesus Christ. I want to let you know one thing about the kingdom; God is very real and so is the other side too.

> "then I saw a great white throne and He who sat on it from whose face the earth and the heaven fled away and there was found no place for them. And I saw the dead small and great stand before God and books where opened and another book was opened which is the book of life and the dead were judged according to their works by the things which were written in the books. The sea gave up the dead who were in it and death and Hades delivered up the dead who were in them. And they were judged each one according to his works. The dead and Hades were cast into the lake of fire this is second death and anyone not found written in the book of life was cast into the lake of fire."

> **Revelation 20:11-15 (NKJV)**

Jesus is the one sitting on the great white throne. Those who will be judged are those that don't believe the Word of God, that blaspheme the word that refused God's salvation in Christ by faith through His grace. Can you imagine the dead ones arising from the sea? We shall be seeing our loved ones again. We will know each other.

The Bible says the sea will give up the dead. In it you can see that no one will be found wanting before the judgement seat. Are you going to be found there? Where are you going to face and what are you going to say to your Maker who made you in His own image? In the likeness of Himself he made you and gave all things to you to enjoy. Do not be outcasts, He loves you. Come back to Him, He will not cast you off no matter how bad you are, He loves you. Remember the life of the prodigal son. He got all his inheritance then went out to lavish all.

After some days, he came back to his senses and went back to his father. The Bible says that his father saw him from afar. That means his father has been longing to see him. What did the father do? He ran and met him on the way, hugged him and welcomed him. Immediately the father called for a party inviting all his friends to come and celebrate with him. A son that was lost but found.

The son had realised his mistake and begged his father for forgiveness. He even went to the extent of offering to return as a servant in his father's vineyard. But his father's reply was "you are welcome I appreciate you are sorry. Just come inside. It is your life that is important to me!" The father called the servants to change all the rags he wore. They put the best robe on him, put a ring on his finger, the seal of ownership.

You are accepted as His, if you can come back home. God's love is constant and welcoming. He will search for every body that was lost by giving us opportunities to respond. Just like the father in this story, His great love reaches out to find sinners out no matter what, why or how they get lost (Luke 15:1-25). Do not be deceived by the devil that blindfolds you with his sweet talk ... "they've been saying it for a long time when is the Lord going to come?" He is a deceiver from the beginning. He will remain like that till kingdom comes. Come out from these lies and sow the seed of your life.

> This is my second letter to you, dear friends. I have tried to stimulate your wholesome thinking and refresh your memory. I want you to remember and understand what the holy prophets said long ago and what our Lord and saviour commanded through the apostles. First, I want to remind you that in the last days there will be scoffers who laugh at the truth and do every evil thing they desire. This will be their argument: *Jesus promised to come back as anyone can remember, everything has remained exactly the same since the world was first created.
>
> 2 Peter 3:1-11 (NKJV)

They deliberately forget that God made the heavens by the word of his command, and he brought the earth up from the water to destroy the world with a mighty flood. And God has also commanded that the heavens and the earth will be consumed by fire on the day of judgement, when ungodly people will perish.

But you must not forget, dear friends, that a day is like a thousand years to the Lord, and a thousand years is like a day. The Lord isn't really being slow about his promise to return, as some people think. No, he is being patient for your sake. He does not want anyone to perish, so he is giving more time for everyone to repent.

With all the truth you've read give your life to him by faith do not harden your heart. A time is coming when you will not have this chance to repent for the grace will cease, for the Bible says "not by power nor by might but by the Spirit of God." If that be the case, you need to repent today for there would be a time you will have to do it by your blood. Then you will not be able to buy or sell without the mark on your forehead, and your hand. satan will require everyone great and small rich and poor slave and free to be given the mark. I am not trying to scare you concerning this, it is written in the book of life and it will come to pass. Revelation 13: 1-18)

This mark '666' stands for incompleteness. It describes evil. Capturing the world and manipulating the people for ungodly ends.

While number seven represents perfection. The books of revelation reveal seven numbers concurrently, seven church's, seven seals, seven trumpets, seven bowls. In the Old Testament we find seven as something that signified the holiness of God. Seven days in creation.

> "So the creation of the heavens and the earth and everything in them was completed. On the seventh day, having finished his task, God rested from all his work. And God blessed the seventh day and declared it holy, because it was the day when He rested from his work of creation.
>
> **Genesis 2: 1-3 (NLT)**

Many rituals were seven fold (Leviticus 4:6,14:15-16, 26:18-21) just to tell you the incompleteness of this mark. This mark will be given by the spirit of antichrist who will come in human body as a peace maker to all the places where there is war especially in the land of Israel. This peace treaty has been going on between many nations, but we know vividly that peace cannot be found anywhere than in Jesus Christ the Prince of peace. Isaiah 9:6. Let us look at what prophet Daniel has for us in his book Dan 9:27 *"he will make a treaty with the people for a period of one set of seven, but after half this time, he put an end to the sacrifices and offerings. Then as a climax to all his terrible deeds, he will set up a sacrilegious object that causes desecration, until the end that has been decreed is poured out on this defiler."*

One set of seven stands as something that sounds good. He always wants to imitate the righteous one. Though it has so many meanings it could be seven years in power to confirm the covenant of peace, but after that many horrible things will happen. Read what (1 Thessalonians 5: 3-4) says "when people are saying, 'all is well; everything is peaceful and secure,' then disaster will fall upon them as suddenly as a woman's birth pains begin when her child is about to be born. And there will be no escape."

Where are you going to turn to? That is why the fourth chapter is telling about not being in darkness once you have had the opportunity of hearing the good news on the radio, television and books like this. Verse four says *"But you aren't in the dark about these things, dear brothers*

72

and sisters, and won't be surprised when the day of the Lord comes like a thief."

Do you remember the story of Noah? The events of Noah's day are a picture of our last days. After Noah, his family and the animals entered the ark the people who had ignored the word of grace that was preached by Noah and given themselves to sin now come to their senses banging on the door of the ark but God himself had shut the door. Understand this simple truth my dear brothers and sisters, the Word of God is true, the day is very near when the Lord will come. Only the redeemed will be with the LORD. The Bible says in Hebrews 9:27 *"it is appointed for men to die once, after this the judgement"* what is your faith in God or yourself?

Take note of this warning, for all have faith in Christ Jesus: the spirit of antichrist has been mentioned in the book of John 2:18 *"little children, it is the last hour and as you heard that the antichrist is coming even now many antichrists have come, by which we know that it is the last hour."*

This spirit will manipulate people's wills and actions to have them bow down for him. The story in Daniel 3:1-30 is about a king who made a golden statue ninety feet tall and nine feet wide and set it in the province of Babylon calling the attention of all people of all races, nations and languages to serve and bow down to his image. He ordered that anyone who refused to obey should be immediately thrown into a blazing furnace. But glory be to God in heaven who has His own people no matter what happens.

There were three young Hebrew men that knew their God. They have been rooted and grounded in the Word of God, established in their faith and given their wills and actions, their whole spirit soul and body to serve Him who lives. We can be challenged by their story: Certain people who were aware of their single commitment to God, were reported to king Nebuchadnezzar.

Look at verses 8-12 *"but some of the astrologers went to the king and informed of the Jews. They said to king Nebuchadnezzar, 'long live the king! You issued a decree requiring all the people to bow down and worship the gold stature when they hear the sound of the instruments. That decree also states that those who refuse to obey must be thrown into a blazing furnace.*

But there are some Jews Shadrach, Meshach, and Abednego whom you have put in charge of the province of Babylon (that was the genesis of the matter, jealousy at the promotion from God motivated this people to bring the report). Listen to this, they have defiled your majesty by refusing to serve your gods or to worship your gods or your gold statue you have set-up."

I want to let you know this, satan will always call you for a fight every time you refuse to bow to sickness, trials, tribulation, loneliness, depression or even compromise in any area of your life. He is always furious at your promotion, but once you know your God he cannot do anything to you by the grace of God.

Shadrach, Meshach and Abednego stood on the Word of God in Exodus 20:4-5 that says "you shall not make for yourself an idol in the form of anything in heaven above or on the earth beneath or in the waters below. You shall not bow down to them or worship them. These three men were given another chance to change their minds but they refused to bow to the god that has mouth and cannot speak, ears but cannot hear. This is the area in our lives where we have to make a quality decision to know who we serve. There are excuses they could have used to justify bowing to the image and saving their lives;

(1) Our position in the society

(2) We are in a foreign land so God will understand that we have to follow the custom of the land and it's just one time after which we can ask God for forgiveness.

The Bible says, *"If you know how to do good and you don't do it's a sin."*

These three lovely brothers were pressured to deny the God of their father but they chose to be faithful to Him no matter what happened! We should be faithful like these men of God to serve with readiness of our heart regardless of circumstances. Our eternal reward is worth any suffering we may have to endure. Though they were judged by the king and thrown into the blazing furnace (he even ordered the furnace to be heated seven times hotter than usual) God delivered them!

There was fourth man in the fire with them, Jesus the king of glory. He has promise us that when we pass through the fire we will not be burned. What a mighty

God we serve! Therefore count it for joy when you fall into any temptation the Lord will see you through. Please don't leave God out of your trouble always cling on.

The beast puts different ungodly things before people in this last age. We must look for the subtle mark of the beast around us and flee.

I want to congratulate the believer in Christ because we are not going to be part of the terrible time. We are going to be with Christ for one thousand years when this beast will take over and cause people to serve him. They will not be able to buy and sell. It will be a terrible time for those that reject Jesus Christ as their Lord and saviour. Today is the day of salvation tomorrow might be too late.

There will be an end to everything. Jesus will put the enemy under his feet then comes the end. He will then deliver the kingdom to the Father that God may be all.

THE COMING OF JESUS CHRIST

The second time of His coming will complete the resurrection harvest and He will subdue all enemies under the Judgment and turn over the divine government to God the Father. The consummation of the covenant will occur when the kingdom is delivered and all the creation will be completely free from all dissident anti-life forces. Once this redemptive task is completed the saving role will be laid aside.

There will be a new earth and a new heaven but sun

will not be needed. satan will be defeated forever and sin will not be found there. All the people of God will live with peace instead of hidden like the day of Adam and Eve. Curses will be removed forever and God will be glorified on earth for the earth will be new.

Revelation 21: 1-8 *"There I saw a new heaven and a new earth, for the first heaven and the earth has passed away, and there was no longer any sea. I saw the holy city, beautifully dressed for her husband. And I heard a loud voice from the throne saying, 'Now the dwelling of God himself will be with men and He will be their God. He will wipe every tear from their eyes, there will be no more death or mourning or crying or pain, for the old order of things has passed away.' He who was seated on the throne said, 'I am making everything new!'*

Then he said 'write this down, for these words are trustworthy and true.' He said to me: 'it is done. I am the alpha and the omega, the beginning and the end. To him who is thirsty I will give to drink without cost from the spring of the water of life. He that overcomes will inherit all this, and I will be his God and he will be my son.

But the cowardly, the unbelieving, the vile, the murderers, the sexually immoral, those who practice magic arts, the idolaters and the liars- their place will be in the fiery lake of burning sulphur, this is the second death.' "

Who are the cowardly the Bible is talking about? They are not those who are weak in faith or doubt or question God in time of trouble or those like Nathaniel (can anything good come from Nazareth?) when not understanding what the scripture says, ask questions.

Rather the Bible is talking about those who turn back from following Jesus Christ.

They are not brave enough to stand for God and turn their back to serve foreign gods. Such are listed among the unbelievers and all the rest but those who can endure to the end and remain faithful will be rewarded. Second death stands for total separation from God. What is your hope? Are you prepared for that or the new heaven? Please answer that for yourself. As God's people we have right to the tree of life.

We will see each other and recognise ourselves in the city called New Jerusalem; a symbol of perfection as was the most holy place (1 Kings 6:1-38). If the earthly temple can be adored how much more the city of perfection. There will be perfect room for the redeemed. The precious materials used in the construction of the city magnify its beauty and glory. It is a place of holiness where everything that sustains life is found (Revelation 22: 8-21).

THE INCOMPARABLE CHRIST

Jesus Christ was born contrary to the laws of life. He was and is and is to come; God Almighty who was in the beginning before the foundation of the earth, who made Himself without any reputation even humbling himself to the point of death even death of the cross. That is why His father exalted him.

He made himself to be poor for you to be blessed. He lived without money in his pocket and possessed neither wealth nor position nor influence. Despite His kingship from above, he started his life as nobody. People did not recognise him but He still loved and saved people healing the multitude without medicine.

He also ruled the course of nature, walked upon the waves as pavement and quieted the sea to stop. He never marshalled an army nor drafted solders nor fired a gun but every knee bows down before Him because of his obedience to God. As I said he never practiced medicine but healed more broken hearts and diseases than any doctors. It is still the same today (Hebrews 13:8).

Remember man is sinful but loved by God, he loves you but hate your sin that is why He is looking for every way to bless you and make your life full and complete. He is offering you not only abundant life here and now but a life which is eternal like his own life.

There is a common saying "no one is perfect we are just human." Yes you are right in a way for that helps us to know our need and acknowledge our incompleteness and separation from God and see that we need him more than we think. He is holy and He is calling us to be holy. Some people would say "I am living a good life, I am giving alms, I am not a murderer, not thinking evil of anybody nor harbour bad motives against anybody." But let it be known today that without man being born again he cannot see the kingdom of God.

You will not see it talk less of entering it. What a pity. Jesus has gone to the cross to take your place before the father and called you his friend. John 15: 13-15 says, "greater love has no one than this, than to lay down one's life for his friends. You are my friends if you do whatever I command you. No longer do I call you servants, for a servant does not know what his master is doing; but I have called you friends, for all things that I heard from my father I have made known to you."

During the course of this book God showed me a dream in which I found myself in a place where there were two people ruling. One was taking people captive and the order loosing them from captivity. There was a lady screaming for help and some people came out and witness to her to go to the Person that set people free and she went. By the time I saw her again she was free jumping and leaping for joy.

The Lord said to me **"anybody whosoever he or she may be, is like that lady."** Bound and crying for help, you might say you don't need anybody's help because you are rich. I am telling you your inner man is calling for help you better answer him now before it is too late. Who was the man that bound people in this dream? It was satan who is their master but you have greater master who is able to set you free without taking anything from you. Salvation is free.

Ho! Everyone who thirsts, come to the waters; you who have no money, come, buy wine and milk without money and without price. Why do you spend money for what is not bread, and your wages for what does not satisfy? Lis-

ten carefully to me, and eat what is good, and let your soul
delight itself in abundance. Incline your ear, and come to
me. Hear and your soul shall live; and I will make an everlasting covenant with you-the sure mercy of David.

Isaiah 55: 1-2,6-7

The sure mercy of David stands for God's mercy and
faithfulness to David, which the Bible applies to life in
Christ Jesus.

Therefore seek the Lord while he may be found, call upon
Him while is near. Let the wicked forsake his way and
unrighteous man his thoughts; let him return to the Lord,
And He will have mercy on him; and to God, For He will
abundantly pardon.

Acts 13:38

Christ Jesus has cried out for justice and has discharged
and acquitted you from the court of the world, only sow
the seed of faith of your life. John 8-36 says, *"If the Son
set you free you are free indeed."* He will start with you and
end up with you the only friend that will not let you
down and not get fed up with you.

You will always fail on your own. Even in him, when
you fall He is not surprised. He knew you before you
were born. He knows your limits. Instead of condemning
you, He will convince you of your sin and seek you until
you repent. He has set a race before you and he will
want you to finish it. He alone can help you.

The race is neither for the swift nor the battle with
spear; the race is by the grace and strength of God. Read

what the Bible says about you *"Remember the former things of old for I am God, and there is no like me, I am God, and there is none like me, declaring the end to from the beginning, and from ancient times things that are not yet done, saying, my counsel shall stand, and I will do all my pleasure, Even to your old age, I am He and even to your grey hairs I will carry you I have made and I will carry, and will deliver you."*

No matter what, you and I will make it once we believe the One called JESUS.

The grace has been giving to us through the blood of Him that was shed on the cross two thousand years ago. Look friend your future is greater than the tempter, he has bright and wonderful at beginning because he started with God before sin was found in him and the wages of sin is death. The devil and his works is doomed but Jesus' kingdom remains and will not end forever Amen.

CONCLUSION

Jesus Christ is the son of God, the Saviour of the world who was moved with love to die on the cross and is now seated at the right hand of our heavenly Father pleading for us day and night. He has gone through all those things you are mourning about.

What you face in life He has faced; rejection, loneliness, pain. Isaiah 53:3 has something to say about Him; "He was despised and rejected by men. A man of sorrows and acquainted with grief." He was oppressed and he was afflicted yet he opened not his mouth. He was led as a lamb to the slaughter taken from prison for judgement.

He suffered great injustice yet open not His mouth. satan tempted him sore the way he tempted Adam and Eve. They both faced the same trial but our Lord passed the temptation because He had a goal. He had a focus and knew where he came from and the purpose of his birth. He knew he was here to destroy the works of the devil. The tempter came with three things; first the lust of the flesh, that is pride of life.

> **so when the woman saw that the tree was good for food that it was pleasant to the eyes and the tree desirable to make one wise; she took of it's fruit and ate. She also gave to her husband (first Adam) with her and he ate.**

> **Genesis 3:6**

Compared with the king of glory I want us to see the game the tempter played with the first and the second Adam. The tree is good for food. The tempter asked the second Adam to command the stone into bread for food when the Word of God in Deuteronomy 8:3 says, *"man must not live by bread alone but by every word that proceeds from God's mouth."* Jesus is the word that proceeds from God's mouth.

Jesus turned his face and rebuked the tempter by his word; the same word God spoke at foundation of the world when He formed the earth. In the early part of this book we were told that sickness, sadness, loneliness, joblessness and death are from the devil. The Bible says satan is the ruler of this earth. Read his statement in the gospel of Luke 4. 5-6: *"the devil took Him up on a high mountain and showed Him all the kingdoms of the world in a moment of time the devil said to Him 'All this authority I will give to you and their glory for this has been delivered to me, and I give it to whomever I wish'."*

Whereas, all power both in heaven and on earth has been given to our Lord Jesus Christ. Glory be to God in the highest. The devil took him up high and said 'this has been delivered to me.' I want you to take notice of this statement from the tempter. 'This has been delivered to me' from who? From Adam and Eve, 'and l give it to whomever l wish.' Verse 7 of the same chapter says, *"Therefore, if you will worship before me all will be yours."*

Note what happened here. satan made his offer as the administrator of the curses on the earth since the first man fell in the Garden of Eden. Notice that Jesus did not contest the devil's right to make that offer of the world and its glory but He pointedly denied, the terms, for their being regained. (Jesus knew he was here to regain all the authority back to his Father).

Therefore do not attribute to God anything of the disorder of our confused, sin and disease riddled, tragic and tormented planet in this present evil age. We are living through all the ages of eternity. Galatian 1:1-5 He died for our sins just as God our father planned, in order to rescue us from this evil world in which we live that is why all glory belongs to God through all the ages of eternity.

Food for thought: Jesus has made himself a ransom for your sins. Do not take foolish decisions by saying 'there is no God' or 'l know but l just can't be bothered' or 'my sin is too big to be forgiven.' Or perhaps you think in your heart 'with all my wealth I don't need God. After all everything is well with me' I am telling you today that you need Him for your life to be meaningful and your sin not to be remembered again.

We can see the love of God for mankind. How wonderful is our God. He causes it to rain on the just and the unjust. Let us take our stand and follow our master regardless of any problem. Jesus has not promised us a trouble free life but He said to us 'I have overcome the world.'

I want you to have this in your mind; as a citizen of kingdom of heaven you will be tempted but it will not overcome you. Therefore don't panic nor give up. Jesus will see you through. Read the letter of brother Paul to the Romans and to all believers. Romans 8:35 *"who shall separate us from the love of Christ? Shall trouble or hardship or persecution or famine or nakedness or danger or sword?" I want to encourage you to stop doubting. God is with you from the beginning to the end of the age Amen."*

When you were dead in your sins and in the uncircumcision of your sinful nature, God made you alive with Christ He forgave your sin having cancelled the written code with it's regulations and laws that stood opposed to you and me, He took it away nailing it to the cross. Therefore as a God's chosen people holy and dearly beloved clothe yourselves with compassion, kindness, humility, gentleness and patience. Do not handle! Do not taste! Do not touch. Separate yourself from evil and you will see the glory of God.

For you that just heard about Christ Jesus for the first time, are you leaving your salvation till tomorrow? What is your reaction to the words of our Lord Jesus, the one who died for your sin? You say "But am not a sinner" I want to let you know that everyone born from woman is a sinner. King David says, *"For I was born a sinner yes from the moment my mother conceived me."*

That is the reason why Jesus said in his word *"unless man is born again he cannot see the kingdom of God that which is born of the flesh is flesh, and that which is born of the spirit is spirit."* See one act of one man brought sin and the penalty is death upon the human race. On the other hand, the obedience of one man counteracted this deed and made righteousness and eternal life available for humankind.

The Bible says all have sinned and fall short of the glory of God that means no one will ever reach God's Holiness without the grace of God through His Son Jesus Christ. Be ready and be convinced in your heart that the Lord has a great plan for you.

The Lord is not slack concerning His promise as some count slackness but is longsuffering toward us not willing that any should perish but that all should come to repentance. Although the wickedness of humankind calls for immediate action, God withholds His righteous wrath and delays judgement for you reading this book to repent.

The coming of our Lord Jesus is at hand and it is going to be sudden. Be prepared. I say again, no matter what you have done He will save you. He alone can fill your emptiness. He forgave the thief at His crucifixion and said to him *"today you will be with me in paradise."* He is saying the same thing to you today. His love is eternal. 1 Corinthians 15:19 says, flesh and blood cannot inherit the kingdom of God but those that believe in Jesus and are born again.

ARE YOU READY TO ACCEPT JESUS CHRIST?

Please pray this prayer with me and your life will not remain the same again.

Father I thank you for giving me your only begotten son Jesus Christ to die for my sins. According to the book of Romans 10: 9-10 that "if you confess with your mouth the Lord Jesus and believe in your heart that God has raised Him from the dead, you will be saved.

For with the heart one believes unto righteousness, and with the mouth confession is made unto salvation."

I believe with my heart and l confess with my mouth that Jesus is raised from the dead today and l declare myself and accept him as my Lord and saviour today. Forgive me all my sin and create a new heart in me. I will follow you for the rest of my life. Come Holy Spirit and help me to live according to your glory, thank you Lord for saving me.

Once you pray this prayer genuinely from your heart you have been saved.

Congratulations you are born into the family of Christ and God's kingdom. Hallelujah praise Lord!

Sing this song with me:

Goodbye world I stay no longer with you I made up mind to go God's way for the rest of my life. I made up my mind to go God's way for the rest of my life.

As you said so it is done in Jesus name,

I make this decision nine years ago and have never for a day regretted doing so. My life has never been the way l was nine years ago. I thank God Almighty for what he has done for me, l was born in a Muslim home but l came to Jesus and he saved me and gave me eternal life which l cannot get anywhere than in Jesus. My life is now secured in Jesus Christ the Lord of Lords and the King of Kings, for the scripture says, *"Whosoever believes on Him will not be put to shame."*

CHAPTER 5

THE NEXT STEP

In 2 Timothy 3:16, Apostle Paul reminded Timothy, that "All Scripture is inspired by God and is useful to teach what is truth and teaches us to realise what is wrong in our lives, it straightens us out and to make one do what is right. Even though the Bible was written hundreds of years ago it's message is timeless, personal and powerful (Hebrews 4-12).

As a result of this by opening the word it gives us encouragement, hope, inspiration and guidance. According to the Bible it is God breathed, you will always find answers to all your need.

1. The first step after been born again is to give yourself to the word that will make you wise. Meditate on the Word of God day and night according to the message God gave to Joshua in Joshua1:8. The Word of God is the gold mine of principles.

Psalms 19:10 says, *"more to be desired are they than gold yea, than much fine gold; sweeter also than honey and the honeycomb."* Memorise the word as a mighty tool against sin; it will even provide immediate availability of God's words as a sword in witnessing and spiritual warfare.

And take the helmet of salvation, and the sword of the spirit, which is the Word of God;

Ephesians 6:17 (NKJV)

Your word I have hidden in my heart, that I might not sin against you.

Psalms 119:11 (NKJV)

2. Find a living church where they preach Jesus Christ, the living, his death and his resurrection. Join them in celebrating what the glorious Lord has done for you. Hebrews 10:25 says, "not forsaking the assembling of ourselves together as is the manner of some, but exhorting one another, and so much the more as you see the approaching." Let the love of God that is shed abroad in your heart lead and move you to please the Lord. Be a clean vessel and ready to live for what you believe.

The palmist says, "*One thing I am asking from the Lord is to stay in the house of the Lord and seek for his glory.*" This king was once a sinner that repented and made a quality decision to serve God and to please Him and he was called a man after God's heart. This is your portion in Him through the help of the Holy Spirit.

As you have made up your mind to follow Jesus don't go back to the same way you use to live. Just depend on the available power he has prepared for those that come to him. He will help you not to make provision for the flesh or lust. Submit to His Lordship by accepting his moral standards, living constantly in fellowship with him, give no room for the devil. He will come so be ready in all season to put the devil back to where he belongs.

He who believes and is baptised will be saved

Mark 16-16

What is baptism? Believing in Christ Jesus is an inward reception while the baptism by immersion is the outward testimony that I have died and been raised with Jesus. My sins have been buried; I am now raised up as a new man in Christ (2 Corinthians 5:17).

Baptism by immersion is different to the baptism of the Holy Spirit. Who is the Holy Spirit? Holy Spirit is a person, a person like Jesus, the third person of the Trinity. The Godhead consist of three divine persons, Father, Son and Holy Spirit each fully God and fully showing the divine nature.

Luke 3:21-22 says when all the people were baptised, it came to pass that Jesus also was baptised; and while he prayed, the heaven was opened. And the Holy Spirit descended in bodily form like a dove upon Him, and a voice came from heaven which said, "You are my beloved Son; in you I am well pleased."

This shows that God the father is the fountainhead of the trinity. The son is the agent of creation and mankind. He was the word that God spoke in the beginning. When God said, "let there be light" and there was light that was Jesus Christ the saviour of the world.

The Holy Spirit is the executive arm of God so He was quite active as God spoke. One has not existed before the other. God the father, Son and the Holy Spirit existed before there was anything. We will understand how it happened when we see our Lord face to face.

In the occasion of Jesus baptism, all three persons were present and active. God the father spoken from heaven, the Son was fulfiling all righteousness, and the Holy Spirit descended upon the Son as a dove. You too must fulfil the righteousness through baptism by immersion and also receive the baptism of the Holy Spirit. You receive power when you receive the baptism of the Holy Spirit. Acts 1:8 says, *"But you shall receive power when the Holy Spirit has come upon you; and you shall be witnesses to Me in Jerusalem, and in all Judea and Samaria, and to the end of the earth."* The life of Jesus conceived by the Holy Spirit and the Holy Spirit in Him brought forth the fruit of good character (Luke 2:52) and later brought forth a ministry of power. You can now see the importance of the power of God. You need this power. l need the power. It is this power that quickens the inspired Word of God, empowers you, convicts you of your sin and always glorifies the father and the son. (John 16:5-15)

When He came upon the disciple of Jesus they were able to do what they could not do before. Jesus knew this before He left them the promise of the coming Holy Spirit.

It came to pass according to the book of Act of the Apostles. Acts 2:1-4 says, *"When the day of Pentecost had fully come, they were all in ONE ACCORD in one place. And suddenly there came a sound from heaven, as of a rushing mighty wind, and it filled the whole house where they were sitting. Then there appeared to them divided tongues, as of fire, and one sat upon each of them, and they were all filled with the Holy Spirit and began to speak with other tongues, as the Spirit gave them utterance."* 'Began to speak' indicates that they continued in the process, in continuation of what Jesus began both to do and teach.

Tongues is an evidence of the baptism with the Holy Spirit either in terms of one's initial experience or one's ongoing life of spirit fullness.

Tongues as a fire, symbolises the presence of God that transforms (Exodus 3:2) When you receive power he will enable you to serve and to witness about the goodness of God. The power of the Holy Spirit is not meant for you to simply sit and enjoy the grace of God for nothing, (Daniel 11:32) but the people who know their God shall be strong, and carry out great exploits.

Once you have the mind of Jesus Christ you will love the word, fellowship with his people this will lead you to prayer. Prayers will lead to praise and worship for who He is not for what you will get from Him. You will praise and worship Him just for what He is and that alone.

Friend please cling to what is holy, pure and worthy of your calling. Now may the God of peace himself sanctify you completely; and may your whole Spirit, soul and body be preserved blameless at the coming of our Lord Jesus Christ, Amen.

CTW PRODUCTIONS

The vision of CTW Productions
is to emphasise your achievement
through goal-setting.

We believe,
if you put your goals in hand of the Lord;
He would give you wisdom and
strength to achieve it.

TO CONTACT THE AUTHOR

Please use the address below:

Modupe Thompson
P O BOX 25097
London SW4 8WP
United Kingdom